MEDICINAL WORDPLAY

Franchesca Collins

ACKNOWLEDGEMENTS

Medicinal Wordplay is dedicated to my grandmother
Evelyn Foster.

Thank you for everything you've instilled me as a child developing into a young woman.

Also, to my father Charles Foster for always being a motivational part of my life.

To my mother Marlene Foster for raising me to be a strong-willed woman with morals and values in order to be successful.

To my mother Marquitta Chisholm thank you for building a better relationship with me after so much missed time.

To all of my brothers and sisters: Dontay, Torrey, Trevin, Stephen, Cashawnah, Shannon, Brittney, and Sylvia.

My cousin Tyshawn.

To every English teacher who had me as a student.

To every poet in the world!

To everyone who has believed in me since day one!

I love you all!

Lastly, thank you God for allowing me to be a chosen one for your people and giving me the gift of writing!

TABLE OF CONTENTS

The Only Chapter

Genius

I escape these bars of imprisonment.

Because life is a gamble isn't it?

Throw my money on the table.

Shuffle my deck of cards.

I'm an ace of hearts but, also an ace of stars.

A winner but, a loser.

A driver and a cruiser.

Always giving you something different.

So you can never say what you're used to.

A goddess but, also an artist.

When it comes to work I put in my hardest.

I write thinking of how it'll end, not how I'm going to start it.

Talent?

No.

This is a gift without a curse.

A poet in her prime.

And a genius in the works.

Forgive Me

Taking these days as they come.

You can make plans but, there's an ultimate one.

Toast these hour glasses.

An hours last is pertinent to this time we all share.

Put these words together for my daughter and my son.

The unborn.

Hoping they are nothing like me.

Something much more.

Thinking of them the most when feeling there's nothing else in store.

Nothing left to gain.

When the waters hit my window pane.

Sitting in a room wishing there was no thing called pain.

Drained.

Four walls.

Held captive.

Driven insane.

Clubs, drugs, and alcohol.

Temptation.

Fornication.

A conformer to it all.

At the computer typing these keys

Suddenly, everything aside on my knees, praying like my prayer just began.

Crying as I'm dying.

Asking God to forgive my sins.

Where Is The Savior?

World is trying and testing me.

Trying to get the best of me.

Trying to live a good life but, niggers not letting me.

I told my mother Marquitta, "I'll see ya when I see ya."

The guilt you have on your heart I wouldn't want to be ya.

Niggers getting' killed left and right.

The skies always grey.

I continually ask my father, "will I see the next day?"

So why can't the sky be blue?

I really don't know.

And why sometimes I feel the way I do, but, my feelings don't show.

And they say time is on my side, when it goes as fast a s a breeze.

And why when someone tells me they're going to do something for me, I find it hard to believe?

Hard dealing with major insecurities.

And how can someone who has never done anything with themselves tell me what's good for me?

Always thinking of situations that are hypothetical.

Lil' sister on the streets because her daddy felt he could let her do what she wanted to.

So, if anything is possible.

Maybe she will someday do a 360.

But, until then I ask that he rides with her instead and not with me.

I know there is a power that is higher.

And there is a woman on your corner right now but, niggers won't buy her.

All the while a mothers kids are hungry, wanting something to eat.

But, she puts that nigger first.

By letting him smash and she ain't getting no cash for the favor.

'Cause if you doing for me and they starving, I'm damn sure goin' pay ya.

Where is the savior?

Can He come down and save this man who's laying on the ground?

'Cause I'm walking past smiling because it's a good day and he has a frown.

Where is the help for people without wealth?

People that are poor and can't do for themselves?

We walk by as if they aren't human too.

But, never stop to think if they're thinking, "what if you were me and I was you?"

And like Cornel West said, race does matter.

'Cause a black who does better than a white pockets ain't fatter.

So, I feel it's time to make changes.

I just need to pack my bags and get away.

This isn't the life for me anymore.

All I have to say.

Nothing

He dropped to his knees not knowing what to expect.

Physically okay.

But, not emotionally in check.

He ‘pose to be in check.

But, can’t seem to write it out.

Mommy didn’t love him and daddy didn’t care.

So, daddy disappeared.

Like the wind he was gone and he didn’t know if he was coming back

He never did.

Crazy he became

So crazily insane.

For what it was worth, he thought it was nothing.

Crack The Sky

Jesus please.

I can't afford this Jesus piece.

These rocks are shining.

Can't help the situation I'm in.

Everything seems like an evolution.

Need a resolution.

Some type of restoration.

The time I'm estimating.

'Cause I've been extremely patient.

Extremely patient?

Yes, to the extreme.

You know what I mean?

Turn to the same page and don't flip back.

I'm on track.

But he's not.

We got to be strong and withstand whatever.

Been through all types of weather together.

Things like tsunamis.

I'm like get away.

He's like soon I'll be away from here if I wait some years.

I hate those tears that I let drop from my eyes.

I no longer despise, or wonder why I go through.

I know you will come down when you feel I can no longer bare.

Heaven I can be so much stronger there.

You're like, "how do you figure?"

'Cause when I look at the sky I see that picture.

Just give me a chance.

I can't look at the heavens from a glance.

But, I will gladly try.

Until you decide to crack the sky.

Life Gambling

She was so gifted but addicted.

Could write anything.

Street life was her story and she lived it.

16.

But looked more like 25.

Put out of her mother's house.

Sleeping with older men was her way to survive.

These men would give her anything from cars to clothes.

To them she was nothing.

Just one of the hoes.

She was smart but, also weak minded.

Looking for love thinking she'd find it in between the sheets.

Her love was so deep for the needles, powder and pills.

So many tried to catch her before she began to fall.

Reaching out, but, she didn't see it all.

Out of the blue her mother died and like never before she got high.

She shared a needle with a man who had full blown.

Lil' Stacy was a teenage girl speeding down a fast lane.

Given AIDS by a man and she didn't know his last name.

I advise y'all to go get tested.

Lil' Stacy could be you.

Same results in a different way.

Taking life for granted huh?

Tomorrow isn't promised just because you're living today.

So Much To Give

Wounds heal but, pain remains on hearts.

Trying to find our way.

Somehow we got lost.

Relying on scriptures that are biblical.

To change our lives and open our minds, our thoughts are critical.

Living on Earth?

This might be heaven.

12 disciples?

There might have been 7.

Jesus died on the cross for our sins but, what about our mistakes?

Trying to feel our way through life.

Saying we love but, demonstrate hate.

What goes up must come down.

Is that really true?

Cause I've been up and down and still most things won't do.

True to religion that's cool and everything.

Send up a prayer and always on the quest of things.

You give not grudgingly but, didn't contribute to offering?

Is that what you're telling me?

We can sing hymns until our lips fall off.

But, remember and not forget we are all lost.

In our flesh.

Depending on our future.

Looking for our past.

We worship our God and worship our cash.

Misery and evil will always clash.

Walking with each other we forget to live.

Going to make a purchase when we are so much to give.

Loss

Blue water and grey skies could never be a couple.

Too many times it was on the tip of my tongue but, I could never say I love you.

Grass never greener on the other side.

Can't say that's true.

I'm here now because you took my love for granted after I trusted you.

Finding love in a hopeless place I'll leave that to Rihanna and Chris.

Although my love is perfect, I can no longer experience this.

I'll just exist in your mind as it clouds you with thoughts.

I know without me you'll be looking to find a way but will always be lost.

Peace be with you.

Consider me a loss.

Under That Fresh What's Left?

I got it.

You know that.

Retro J's, KD'S, with the Tru's and Polo for days.

Under that fresh you still have your ways.

Lost as a boy, so your priorities were never prioritized.

As you hid behind those lies.

Or should I say those Prada shades?

And you have aged into a man who's primarily concerned with the materialistic side of lie.

Women only see you as having it.

So what about a wife?

You never even let that cross your mind.

Your daddy was a loser, domestic abuser, drug use.

He never taught you how to be a man.

Step inside a chuch door.

All you know is Dior, Cavalli and Fendi.

Have you ever asked yourself what's within me?

Do I possess substance?

I want to know love but, no potential to be a husband.

Go to the club with a label on that's purple.

Just like you these women have no intentions on loving but, indeed they'll hurt you.

Your Nikes and socks designed as being elite.

Funny, you'll find your heart and your soul sometimes at your feet.

That check says, "just do it" and that check says "just spend it."

One day you'll look back and say, "what was I thinking?"

Sitting in a fresh Mercedes.

Under that fresh what's left?

God to judge me and another man to hate me.

Same niggers who never understood me but, shook hands saying they can relate to me.

A boy stuck in a man's skin.

Yes, I hide behind my flesh and use my fresh as happiness.

What's under has been my weakness.

Running.

Racing against odds, when there's no cheating them, I'm fresh.

Mental development is still as important as an adult to me as it was when I was a child. Watch your surroundings and the people you are around. If they can't teach you anything, they're worthless. If you're not growing, you're dying. Don't die now.

You Can Do Better

Been together 10 years.

Slapped around for six.

How can you say that's love?

More like bullshit.

I'm your friend, so I'll keep it real.

Love isn't how you wear it.

More so how you feel.

That lipstick and foundation is just a cover.

You are the book.

Judging others takes a second look in that glass that displays your reflection.

Protect yourself.

Use your heart as a weapon.

Mind tells you to stay.

Why is it you're neglecting the woman you used to know?

Maybe because he does everything for you financially.

You think if you were to leave, he would care?

I mean answer me.

No, no.

Never mind.

In time you will come across the girl you used to know.

So long ago when you weren't lost and had the potential to be the girl I am today.

Standing strong on her own two.

You can do better.

Better has to start with you.

Let Me Know

You have me sometimes perplexed.

Not knowing what to expect.

I think you are the person I have yet to know.

Don't be afraid to show me how you really feel.

Just be for real and you will feel so much better.

I don't know whether we are on the same page or not.

Eventually you'll make that evident.

I'm going to try to pace it.

I like you so hard.

Take it how you want to take it.

If you don't feel the same way as a result, then that means I wasted your time.

You can say it's my fault.

You told me that you would rather not take it there.

We took it there unexpectedly.

So, having no control, should we let that be?

I think so.

I'll be waiting so let me know.

Generation X

2015.

A year to progress.

No remembrance of the past.

Just a list of regrets.

Youth described as being generation X.

Can’t read or write, but, can lay down for sex.

Go to school, but, are incapable of passing standardized tests.

What happened to advancement?

Black excellence now up in the air because youth

lack unity and the idea of going somewhere.

The big picture has become much smaller.

Young boys and girls addicted to street life and that’s what they call love.

Broken homes have amounted to these broken hearts.

Speech patterns profane due to poor vocabulary.

Not used to picking up books.

This generation knows nothing about a dictionary.

City schools in and everyday uproar.

Teachers teach for their checks but, aren't encouraging students to want much more.

When it's time to read between the lines of symmetry they don't know the math because the lack teacher to student chemistry.

If the children thought beyond what they can only imagine, that thing that they want today, they'll look up tomorrow and have it.

Times are harder than anyone can see.

It doesn't take a scientist to notice.

We speak of being hopeful but, forget about the hopeless.

The youth.

Living just because.

Not fulfilling their destinies through being focused.

It's a cold world for generation X.

Don't allow your child to be a factor.

Yes we can progress together.

Call It My Gene

Determination can be infinite.

Never put it to a cease.

Writing is a mental stimulation.

Having its own release.

Of thoughts today, tomorrow, and many days after.

Neglected by its loved ones it is its only attention.

Capturing minds across the globe.

Its most high intention.

Jumping off pages and into your souls.

Onto the stage and into the spotlight.

No time to blink.

Words take control of everything from the floor to the ceiling.

To behind the scenes.

That's why I write.

Born with words.

As I pass them on.

Call it my gene.

A Change Will Come

And with the old comes the new.

You can make it out but can you make it through?

You can concentrate but, what's your concentration?

You can separate yourself and be a part of the situation.

Be a solution as well as the problem.

Doing what you want.

Not pursuing what you need.

Planting for growth never, starting with a seed.

Planning your life looking behind you and never ahead.
Try and you fail.

So, you give up instead.

Looking for what seems so far away.

A change will come.

You have to want it today.

Against My Vows

If I could I would take that back.

If you could you would forgive me for doing that.

Treat me like you did before.

Love me like you did before Satan came knocking at our

front door trying to break up something so happy.

Our home.

Tearing us down when it took everything to build these walls.

From ground up we accomplished trust.
Trust didn't last too long.

Conforming to lust.

On late nights and early mornings coming home in the same clothes
I had on yesterday.

Had the nerve to lie next to you.

I had gone against my vows.

Now there's nothing left to do.

Others Expectations

People sometimes expect you to live your life the way that they want you to.

You think, I can only live for me.

I think that you're absolutely right.

I surely don't want to know what living up to someone else's expectations is like.

I get over this being under and I wonder.

He Always Answers

About my business so I mind it.

Trying to find myself.

Looking past what's in front of me into the invisible.

Poetry is spiritual.

Looking to uplift you.

When I pick up the ink it is uplifting.

A gift so remarkable.

I'm forever grateful.

Thanking my God for my potential asking that I go far.

Pick up the phone every day and He always answers my call.

Faith

And with all the questions came answers.

Project girl.

Goals and a dream deferred living with cancer.

Baby boy at age 16.

Dropped out and pursued her GED.

Times were hard because the doctors had no cure for what seemed to be the end of her life.

Plugged up in hospital rooms more than she saw daylight.

She wanted to obtain a bachelor's degree in science so she studied online.

Praying every day that she doesn't flat line.

And of course for her the struggle was unbearable.

But, she had gotten her strength from her mother.

It was inherited.

Her hair was gone but not her will to survive.

The crying at night and breakdowns was only a part of her drive.

A part of her strive for greatness.

When the people around gave up on hope she said, "I can take this."

When she was alone most nights in a dark room crowded with fears,

pillows drenched from tears.

Weight loss from stress.

Jesus was her only friend because through it all he saw the best.

Studying when she was so weak.

A patient of this epidemic for three years and two weeks.

She's now 22 and three weeks away from May 17th.

Her graduation day.

She went into remission all because she didn't just talk to God.

She also listened when He said that He would and to have faith.

So she did.

May 17, 2003 she walked across the stage cancer free.

Never say that you can't.

Just go after.

Nothing's impossible.

2005 she also received her master's.

Claimed

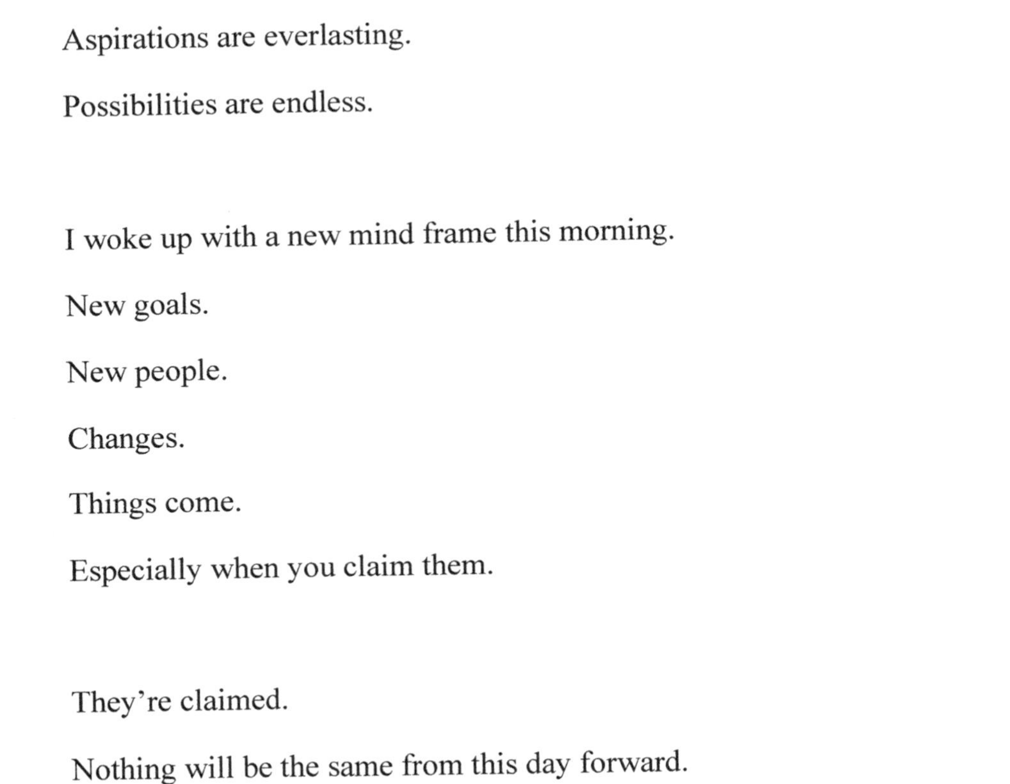

Dreams come true.

Aspirations are everlasting.

Possibilities are endless.

I woke up with a new mind frame this morning.

New goals.

New people.

Changes.

Things come.

Especially when you claim them.

They're claimed.

Nothing will be the same from this day forward.

No looking back over my shoulder.

I've realized that time is divided between the young.

I mature much more as I become older.

By Storm

Crossing my mind are x amount of thoughts.

True to the game.

Give my heart and soul.

Thought love had my back.

Cole.

Love is blind.

Eve.

Never knew you had tricks up your sleeve.

Wish I could put it in a love song.

Keys.

But, I put it in a poem.

My feelings just hit me by storm.

Chasing a pavement.

Adele.

I pack my bags and be a lady.

Badu.

Mad as hell.

I trusted you.

Someone's sleeping in my bed.

Dru.

I just died.

Amerie.

Lost for words.

I hope you have nothing left to say to me.

Farewell

No need to complain.

Heartbroken.

Wounds too deep.

Too many thoughts on the brain.

Try but fail to obtain goals on my plate.

Drive but then brake.

Always real.

Always come across fake.

Don't want to be around lames.

They should be ashamed of not who they are, but, what they haven't become.

Feeling hypocritical.

I mean I ought.

It's not what you know but how you've been taught.

So I ride or die.

Cry and strive.

Tears never hit my feet.

Creeping through the darkness.

On this uphill battle.

Damn it is steep.

Too much time has been spent on foes who came but have gone their own separate ways.

By myself.

Experiencing many hectic days.

Haven't slept in days.

Where is there time for sleep?

Only defeat is the reflection in the mirror.

Everything is clearer as I escape hell and am released from my cell.

No longer in my shell.

Only time will tell the story.

As I embrace my past with a farewell.

The Difference

Can't judge the people around while they're judging me.

I can only observe myself and think of possibilities.

Doing right.

No wrong.

It's like I'm gone.

But, I'm still here in a room where I'm the only person who's different.

Can I chill here?

Hell yeah.

That would be my prize.

Knowing that it's difference that I can no longer despise.

It's Only Right

You were thinking of me.

That put a smile on my face.

At the same time in the back of my mind I'm asking how to erase memories from years ago.

I don't know.

Maybe we can change each other.

You are so attractive in many ways.

Together I hope we can spend many days and that those days turn to nights.

I want to see you first in the morning.

It's only right.

As A People

You would think as a people we would be supportive of each other.

MLK Jr. wrote "I Have A Dream" so that I could sit down with my own brother.

Times have changed only in some places.

Some blacks and whites still hate to acknowledge each other's faces.

Let alone races.

History from the ships of Africa bringing us over.

Voyages to make us stronger and have us all unite as one.

Whether in a mansion on a hill or residing in the slum.

It's only our skin color people.

Look around and treat your brother equally.

All I Got

Times like these I wish I had someone that could ease the pain.

Keep me sane.

Ever since my last, I don’t think that I can love again.

Things are strange.

Not being able to sleep at night.

You’re not here anymore.

Do you think about what my life is like?

The reason in the morning I rose.

Now I’m like whatever and anything goes.

I cry whether the tears are visible or not.

Don’t think I’ll ever stop.

Don’t know if you knew but, you’re all I got.

Changes

The sun is shining but, I am crying.

My heart is broken into too many pieces.

Can you see it?

Got to put it back together.

Get my act together.

Look past all these insecurities.

Getting the best of me is my immaturity.

Got to stay strong and be much clever.

Make a change that's drastic.

I always needed this one question to be answered but, I never asked it.

What is in this life possibly that I can see to benefit me positively?

All I try to be is something.

Nobody can't tell me nothing.

I'm always the one that's fronting like I don't need peoples help.

I can't do for myself.

I just need a serious motivation.

Tired of just sitting around and waiting.

It's really becoming too frustrating.

I find myself always debating whether one day I should just hop out of bed

and take a look in my mirror.

Maybe things will be so much clearer.

Then the doors will open up.

I refuse to trust the fact that things will come around to me.

Killing It

Conscience is killing me.

Facing possibilities, I know are possible to undergo.

Sometimes I don't know but, I don't show my inside on the out.

I don't want others to figure me out just that easily.

I want to them to think, "Oh yeah that girl right there needs to be a part of a major concentration. A crazy concentration that's out of this world."

Have people appalled and in awe because I did the possible when I thought impossible.

Now get me to a hospital.

The skills are sick.

Real real sick.

On some real real shit, I'm getting it together.

Even though it's strange to not change but, rearrange this game of life.

Looking forward and not back.

I've learned and I've earned my right to show you.

Beneficial

Do you know that since we have been as one,

I feel that in my heart there's a place for you bigger than the sun.

I can't describe this love.

It's unconditional.

I being with you has been the best thing for us and for me beneficial.

I don't know what you are doing to me but this feels so good.

You being the one I give myself to is to whom I think I should.

If you ever leave me I will deeply miss you.

I being with you has been the best thing for us and for me beneficial.

You make me feel that in this world we are Adam and Eve.

Where things begin.

I just can't see me without you.

In my book that's a sin.

I love you.

To me you are more precious than any diamonds, pearls or crystals.

I being with you has been the best thing for us and for me beneficial.

Prime Time

Mind over matter.

Thoughts over heart.

Time I wish I had you.

So I'd know where to start.

Put an end to this beginning.

Things seem so simple at times.

At times things are too complex.

Hating to remember those things we want so bad to forget.

Pick up this pen.

Never put it to the paper.

I put it to the test.

To reach out to those who aren't able to express

their gratitude for things written and the best in its making.

For you to remember these poems is all that I'm asking.

Now and for the remainder of my time.

I respect you took the time to read.

From the best.

In my prime.

Happiness

You can have everything and still be miserable.

Happiness with yourself is critical.

Stay within yourself.

I look in the mirror and stare at my reflection.

Not just that but my perfection.

Not just human but a blessing.

Born July 16, 1987.

24 years ago.

You're reading but it's imperative that you hear me though.

I'm going to do it all before my death date.

I love the hate and appreciate the love.

Shout out to my number one.

God above.

Hard To Express

Can I be your stimulation mentally, emotionally and physically?

Better yet, how about spiritually?

Make you feel uplifted when strength can no longer lift you up?

Try with you when it is yourself on whom you have given up?

Make you smile when it's been so long you've had a frown on your face?

At the end of each day make you feel that it's me you want to embrace?

Allow me to show you something different because it's apparent you're used to the same thing.

Open up your heart and mind.

Explore the unexplainable.

Help you reach goals that you didn't believe were attainable.

See things from a birds' eye view.

Together me and you.

There are no limitations to what we can do.

Have faith in what I'm asking because it's nothing but real.

I only wrote this for you because face to face it's hard to express exactly how I feel.

Truth Hurts

If a heart could shatter like glass, could the future be a representation of the past?

The question is a trick on the mind only to find we are the text of the books, but never read between the lines.

If our signature is a sign of consent, could we erase time and say that time was never spent?

You see life is like a game of chess.

Once the wrong piece on the board is moved you lose because when it came to thought, you never gave thought your best.

Sometimes we seek to restrain pain although pain is displayed on the face.

When we look around we can't look at each other and know the time nor place

things changed for the worse.

If life were a play would you rehearse?

Play your part well because in life the good vs. bad and happy vs. sad coincide.

Coming from a thought provoked individual.

Take your pride and stride.

When it's time to put it aside.

Truth hurts but, it's better than living a lie.

Alone I Will Stay

Truthfully this is the new me.

Can't shake me?

I thought you were so through with me?

Now you're calling me again.

I don't want to be called.

You're trying to see me.

Knocking and I don't want to answer.

Get away from my door.

You must don't understand that you aren't welcomed anymore.

Do me this favor and just stay away.

I can do better alone.

Alone I will stay.

Describe It

Walking these empty hallways.

No one around.

The only one here to make a sound.

In a deep water.

Can't swim but, I fail to drown.

On this bridge and out of the hall.

What is it you saw?

Could you describe it?

Let's see.

When we're together again.

Just you and me.

Out Here

Out here in the cold.

Wind blowing.

Mind gone.

What's my next move?

I have to figure that out.

Doing my thing every day.

You already know what it is.

I stopped shining.

Just grinding.

Truthfully.

Doing Without

Attempts turn into things getting done.

If it's done there's no turning back.

People only come around when your life is on track.

When you're down and out they won't even give you a call.

One thing I've realized in a short period of time is that people are really for seasons.

I don't have the time.

Doing without.

I'm fine.

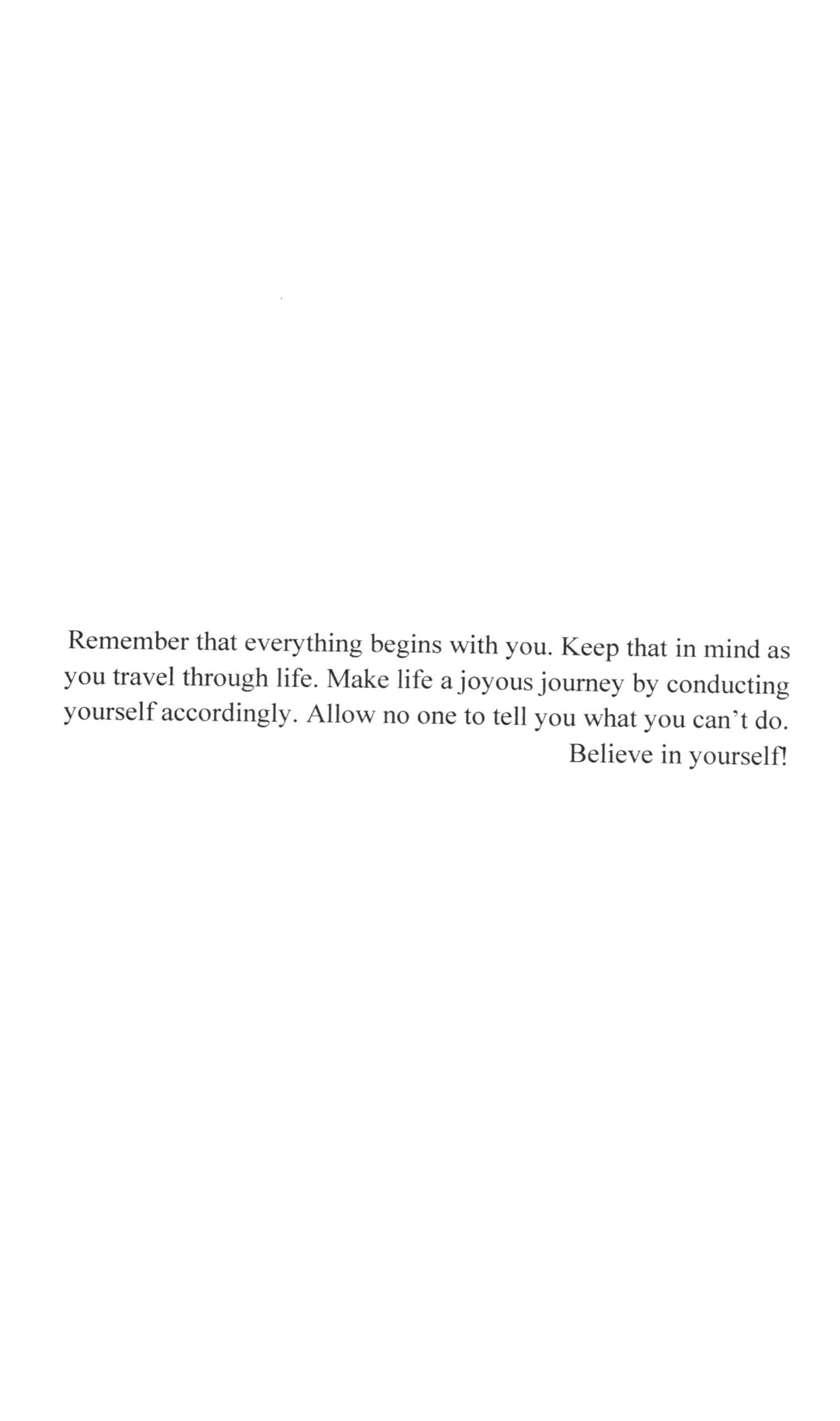

Remember that everything begins with you. Keep that in mind as you travel through life. Make life a joyous journey by conducting yourself accordingly. Allow no one to tell you what you can't do. Believe in yourself!

Racism Is Still Alive: Dedicated to Trayvon Martin

Can't walk down the street without being perceived.

A threat to society being black.

So hard to believe.

Young but stride alone.

Driven but the ride is lonely.

Sometimes it is hard to accept the truth.

Reality is that things aren't changing amongst our youth.

As adult facing reality along with these fears, comes the question.

Is racism still alive after these hard fought years?

Yes.

It is believed from the heart.

Especially when our brothers so close but so far away are being shot and killed with no justifications in America today.

As a nation we remain weary with no guidance.

When our brothers are slain because they're black, so many speak but, still there's an awkward silence.

Trayvon Martin is down in the books.

Innocent and black.

Racism is still alive each day you leave your home.

That's a fact.

Could Care Less

Kissed me yesterday.

No respect for me today.

Wasn't informed love could be lost overnight.

Here's the experience.

Thought you had sense.

Why leave me delirious.

I'm sorry that I wasn't what you wanted me to be.

I'm just myself.

You forgot who was there for you when there was no one else.

Running your mouth.

Could care less.

Let it run.

Cause the grass is never greener on that other side.

She's just for fun.

Come Back

I know I said we wouldn't work.

As time went on I couldn't embrace the hurt with my mind or my heart.

Gone.

Wish that we could start again.

My friend whom I really want to be my lover.

I don't know how to let you know.

So, I play everything off like you don't mean too much to me.

Mouth closed and that sucks for me.

I refuse to dwell on the situation too long.

I can accept the fact that I did even though I said I'd never do you wrong.

I wish I could kiss you as I'm writing this.

In my feelings all over again and I'm not liking this.

Come back.

Stand Tall

Weakness will be sometimes although the times are seldom.

Others will not offer with open arms a sincere welcome.

Be open minded.

A mind closed shall never be exposed or withhold thoughts from others around.

When being taken advantage of, hold your ground.

Take in others opinions.

For opinions lead to pacing observations and embracing knowledge.

Knowledge is key to demonstrating your best, better and worse.

Every time you have found a relief upon release, put everything you have grasped in life to a test.

Things will work.

Until

Hold on tight.

We're on a ride.

Not alone but together.

Not just for now but forever.

The last person you see at night is me.

All day on my mind is your kiss.

Your touch.

Miss you much when you're not in my presence.

Can't smile if you're not smiling.

Can't think of any other place I'd be.

If there wasn't a you, I wouldn't be the best person I can be.

Thank you.

Years have been.

Years to come

We will be until our lives are done.

Just In Time

Truth is that we never know what tomorrow brings.

So I live for today and let go of things that really don't matter.

Hold no grudges with others.

We all die but aren't guaranteed to see each other in the next life.

Time on Earth is just time.

In heaven there are no clocks.

Every angel moves freely.

I wish it was like that here.

Not 24 hours in a day.

No specific times to wake up each day.

You don't work in heaven.

You just relax.

If there is work, better believe God ain't taking out taxes.

We get what we put in, in everything we do.

So when your time is over, you don't need a watch.

No time in heaven.

Just in time.

Space

Dreaming.

Eyes are open.

Skepticism is a reality.

When doing something you've never done, follow through or fall off.

Giving up shouldn't be an option but if you've given up get back to what you know.

No one knows you better than you and God.

Through trials and tribulations there's always space to grow.

Hurry

Can't seem to wake up.

Who would've seen this break up coming.

Everything just happened so fast in a flash.

My past you are.

Thought you were a star that would never drift across the sky.

I'm lost.

Why?

Who knows.

I turn to those who really love because you really didn't.

If you did, you should've taken things as they were.

It shouldn't have made a difference who my friends were or who didn't like you in my family.

I told you from the start that I wanted you to be all you can to me.

You weren't.

You still don't think that you're wrong.

I still don't think that you're gone because I feel you'll be back.

We'll see if the next compares.

Nothing left but cares.

I'm no longer worried.

Consider this your last walk out of my door.

Grab your box.

Hurry.

Owe Her

I put my money on it and put my mind away.

I put a hundred on it and put my nine away.

My niggers like, "No just spray."

I got a daughter to feed.

Feel like I'm falling.

Sort of like a leave.

Just without the color.

Living without a father or a mother, I feel like I owe her.

Just ought to show her what a good life should consist of.

My whole life I just wished for love.

Can't

Treated you like an angel.

You couldn't handle that.

Wasn't I good enough?

Baby answer that.

Real unfair that you were unable to see that you were cutting me up internally.

Sure I wanted us to last but evidently you didn't.

If so you wouldn't have gotten that close to her or let her get that close to you.

You're saying that you didn't.

Don't lie now.

I already heard the truth.

"Heard the truth?"

Yes, that's what I heard from you.

So, now it's over.

There is no coming back.

I'll just let you go.

I can't.

Dark and Lonely

Asleep.

When will I awake?

Not much time to stand on Earth.

My heart is the quake.

I better find your loving.

Drake.

Never knew this could be an attack on my heart.

Songz.

I don't want to hear any more songs.

Tired of these Mr. Wrongs.

Blige.

I can't afford any more cries.

You should let me love you.

Mario.

I walk around teary eyed because the clouds block the sun which will display my rainbow.

Let's make beautiful music.

Cole.

That music I had became played out and it's old.

To the left?

I want you on my right.

How can I awaken from this dream I’m having of you on this dark and lonely night?

Locked Heart

It's when I'm alone that you cross my mind the most.

For some reason I can't shake you.

I think it's because we were so close.

Now it's strange because everything I've done to you is slowly coming back.

You say that nothing was there, so I can't say I want that back.

I can only say this one thing.

Although I see you physically, at the same time my conscience is killing me.

I have everything I need.

I'm sorry that it's not you.

You took the key and locked your heart.

How can I get through?

Unsure

Brand new on this paper is this ink.

Brand new are these thoughts.

I begin to think of the future and where I lay my head.

When I say that I don't mean bed.

I mean on the streets of life.

How can I expose the real me?

Wait a minute.

I know not my own identity.

I think I'm this way.

Society views me as another.

So, do I go by the opinion from that of my brother?

I don't know the answer but, that I shall find.

I can't predict or see the future.

I'm leading the blind.

We are on a path together.

Whether the path is straight or whether it will take a turn we are unsure.

We shall learn.

If You Were Her

Rhymes from times like these I wish I had some.

Niggers who got laid down wish they had guns.

Which is an unfortunate situation.

Four years straight been court casing.

In and out the penitentiary.

Wouldn't have been like that if had been a friend to me.

A friend?

Yeah.

Like no other.

I had no mother, no father.

Didn't bother to fight and be like them because if it wasn't for him I wouldn't have this scar on my chin.

Yeah my daddy hit my mommy on the daily.

It always scared me.

I thought he might kill the only person I loved.

I never held a grudge.

But, he was like a stranger.

I held back this anger for way too long.

Days too long.

So I carry on as if life is a never ending breeze.

I don't think I ever can believe that he was my daddy.

Yeah the one that made me.

Lord please end this pain because I don't think I can take this shit no more.

Not even if a nigger paid me or traded me with another life.

'Cause I love her to death.

There's no other left to trust or rely on.

I tried forgiving daddy by letting bygones be bygones.

I can't see no more.

Feels like my eyes are gone.

So, what is my song?

Hell if I know.

But, I do know one thing though.

What goes around always comes back.

Hitting mommy he had always done that.

She would forgive but never forget.

Neither did I.

We knew she was being deceived and lied to.

So, one day I'm going to say to daddy, put yourself in mommy's shoes.

Think what you would do if you were her and she were you.

The White Lady

On the come up from the down of things.

I always listen to this one song for the sound it brings.

People think we make the world go 'round, when really it's the paper.

To that paper I'll do anything to make you.

To my love I just can't seem to shake you.

I say forget the bullshit even though at times I hate you.

Can't seem to find my concentration or concentrate on the most important shit.

I'm hating it.

I rely on something so pure.

She's white and I'm black.

We get along well.

She completes me when shit else can't.

So I hit her one last time and that was goodbye.

Noticing The Problems

The problems will never cease.

Living in a city with one of the highest crime rates in the nation, I really hate to acknowledge the problems that the people are facing.

Killing each other over who knows what.

The murder rate has decreased a little but still hasn't been cut.

Who is responsible for this and who can we blame?

What we need to notice is that noticing the problems will never be a game.

As I Walk

Sacrificing the only thing I have.

Life.

As I walk through school impervious to others who

want to bring out the evil spirit they hope to see.

I think about a lot of things and incumbent me.

Who is this person?

Do I know her?

Never influenced anymore to do as others would have me to do.

Realizing the highest of all of my potential.

Only worried about my eye and I.

Never no more worried about you.

As I walk.

Questions

Do I have to be the one who draws attention?

Or can I just be the one who no one cares about or even thinks to mention?

Can I just be one who speaks to only those with whom I associate?

Or speak to those I don't know, want to love and never to hate?

Is it my personal self that only I should know?

Or, should I let others in so that I know which way to go.

Is it I that everyone wants to eye and look my way?

Or, is it I who is looking for a brand new day?

Her So Called Love

She thought she ought to love anyone who had the personality of the stars above.

He abused her but, yet in the midst of it all he used her.

She didn't know that her heart was being broken.

Still there were some words she felt that were still unspoken.

It was like she knew what was happening.

Then, the next day she found that she was going to be unhappy.

Unhappy with the so called love of her life.

She even thought that one day she would become his wife.

She was thinking, "Why me? Why must anger live inside of me?"

"I need to move on but, yet my feelings for him are so strong. What he is doing to me is so dead wrong."

From now on I will still wonder if he loves me anymore.

I don't care I'll just let him walk out the damn door.

Unexplainable

It's something I can't explain.

You're the person I run to whenever my heart is in pain.

I feel at peace whenever I hear your voice or see you.

I always want to be the one you love.

I love you.

If someone else tried they couldn't be you.

I try being to you the best person I can be.

I feel that you are the reason I awake, smile, breathe or eat.

I never knew another human that's so sweet.

You're forever mine.

Always on my mind.

Whenever I sleep I dream and it's always about you.

Forever we will always be.

I love you so much and there's no doubt in my mind that you love me.

Sometimes

Sometimes I feel like in this world I have no purpose.

Or, that I'm the only human on the planet walking its surface.

I can't help these feelings that are being felt.

Maybe you're the only person I can turn to for help.

You do it well.

Make me feel that things last forever.

Always letting me know you're there and that loving me is something you want to endeavor.

My song of songs.

Love.

The one I turn to other than the Lord above when things are right and when they're wrong.

Please be there for me always.

I'll let my affection be shown.

You're my voice.

My everything.

My Pen

So as I grabbed my pen and began to write, I reflected upon what a joyous life should be like.

I really don't know but I know what I would want it to be.

I would want someone to love me unconditionally.

Not for my possessions.

Simply me.

Someone to take things slow.

When I have problems I don't have to tell them.

They already know.

When my feelings are hurt, I go to them and simply cry.

Even if I'm crying and don't know why.

All I Got

Times like these I wish I had someone that could ease my pain.

Keep me sane.

Ever since my last, I don't think I can love again.

Shit is strange not being able to sleep at night.

You're not here anymore.

Do you think about what my life is like?

The reason in the morning I rose.

Now I'm like whatever and anything goes.

I cry whether the tears are visible or not.

Don't think I'll ever stop.

Don't know if you knew but, you're all I got.

The Way It Seems

Sitting here with my pen and pad.

Feeling disgracefully sad.

Thinking of a good life.

Something I wish I had.

Times like these I wish I had a friend.

That person I can depend on.

I thought about hope but, hell that's been gone.

Can I get that back?

Yes, that love thing?

Yeah you know what I mean.

Come back to me and it really won't be the way it seems.

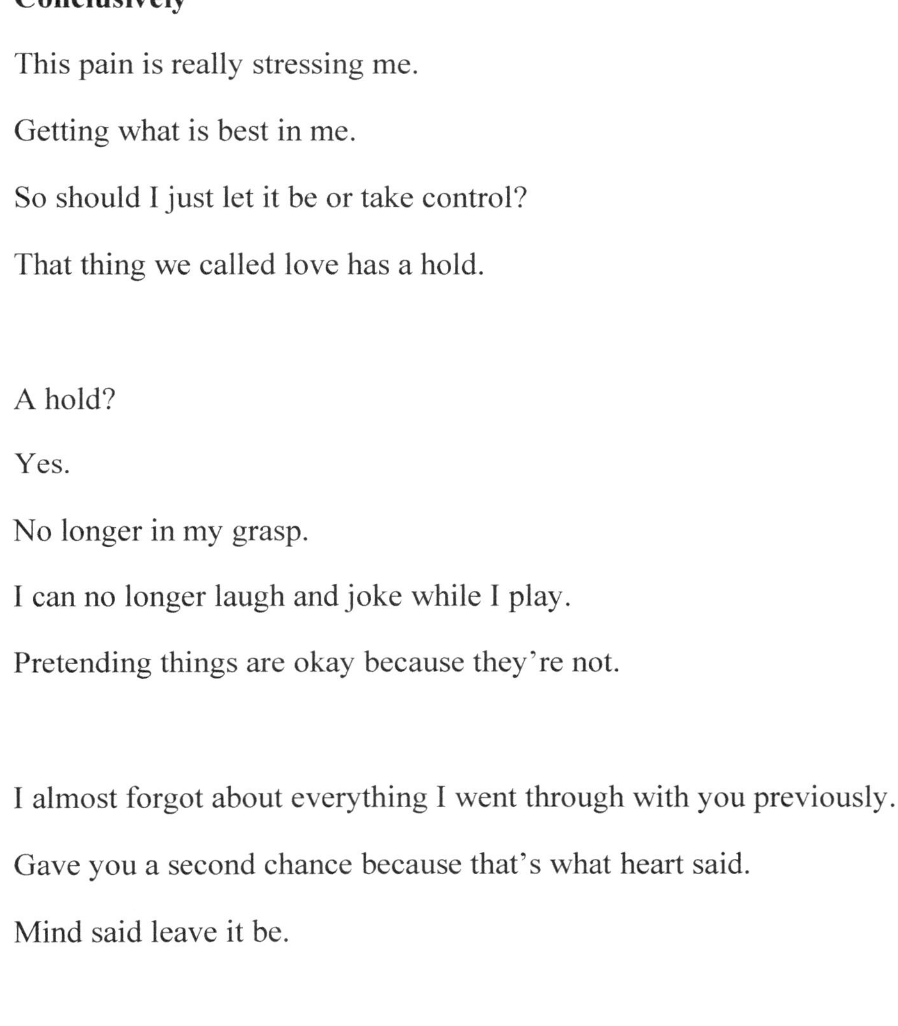

Conclusively

This pain is really stressing me.

Getting what is best in me.

So should I just let it be or take control?

That thing we called love has a hold.

A hold?

Yes.

No longer in my grasp.

I can no longer laugh and joke while I play.

Pretending things are okay because they're not.

I almost forgot about everything I went through with you previously.

Gave you a second chance because that's what heart said.

Mind said leave it be.

Second chance came back to haunt.

No matter how you put it you don't want what you once had.

In a way I'm glad.

You taught me the best lesson I could ever be taught.

Never trust someone who has done someone in their past wrong.

They'll do it you with no hesitation.

I was hesitant and patient.

It hit me like a hollow tip.

I swallowed it.

Conclusively.

On My Mind

You're on my mind much more than myself.

I stare at your picture sometimes.

Your eyes I can't help what they do to me.

I'm tired of old Franchesca.

I want you to be the one who brings out the newer me.

I wonder if you ever notice my admiration for you.

It's strong.

I want you to be all I got.

Love you every day and find it hard to not.

Die cold side by side in graves.

Lovely deaths.

Together our flesh shall rot.

I Love You

I love you because of your mind.

You take the time to share thoughts with me.

Never would've thought we'd be, but, we are.

For you I stand tall with no intentions of falling down.

I walk with my head held high.

You are my ground but, I'll never walk over you.

When you're not around I always wish it was you I am closer to.

Dedicated to: M.L.W

Drink In My Hand

So I'm walking down the street with a drink in my hand.

Then, I stopped not knowing what to think as I stand on this corner.

In life everyone's born a sinner.

As I sip, this bottle has me captivated.

I think about these trying times and life itself realizing that I hate it.

Nothing comes for free but a courtesy cup of water.

It's hurting that I'm stuck.

I got to look out for my daughter.

I'm so twisted now that the bottle hit the concrete.

I don't hear anything else around but my own heartbeat.

I can spend money on being fresh to death but, I can't buy a weekly bus pass.

Ain't that some mess?

I just got to make it like Trey.

So I'm hustling hard trying to be the ace of my hood.

Take a look at my life.

Mary J.

What would you say?

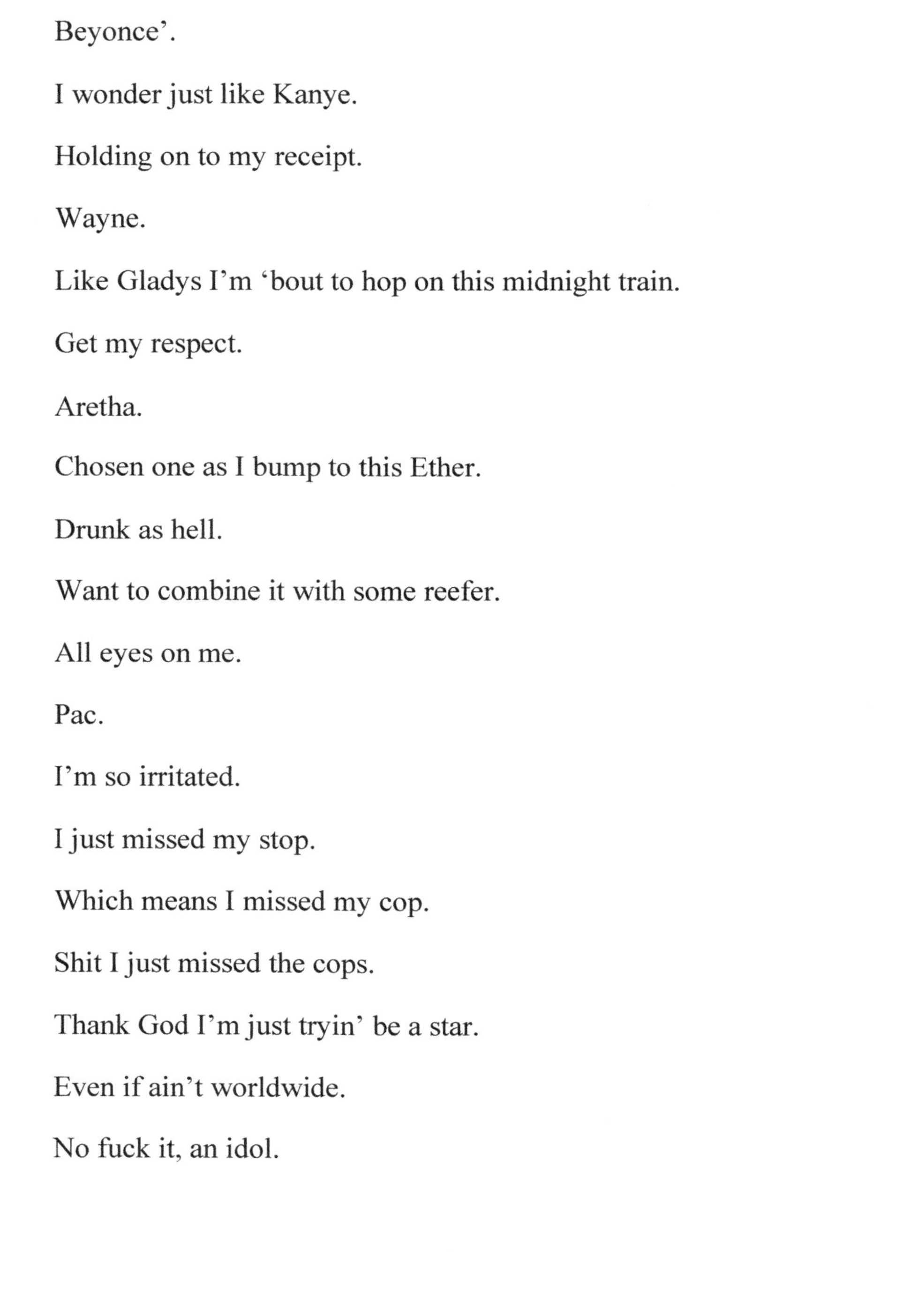

Probably nothing.

Speechless.

Beyonce'.

I wonder just like Kanye.

Holding on to my receipt.

Wayne.

Like Gladys I'm 'bout to hop on this midnight train.

Get my respect.

Aretha.

Chosen one as I bump to this Ether.

Drunk as hell.

Want to combine it with some reefer.

All eyes on me.

Pac.

I'm so irritated.

I just missed my stop.

Which means I missed my cop.

Shit I just missed the cops.

Thank God I'm just tryin' be a star.

Even if ain't worldwide.

No fuck it, an idol.

Jennifer.

Girl keep calling me.

I tell her like baby I'm really not that into you.

On every sidewalk you'll find squares.

I start back at one.

McKnight.

Time to lay my ass down.

Last thought.

Goodnight.

Poem Cry

Mommy is that you on the kitchen floor high again?

Is that me at the kitchen table attempting not to cry again?

I'm nine.

But, I feel like I grew up already.

I don't want to have to watch my siblings today or clean the house.

I just want you to get me ready for school just one time before you're out.

I'm tired of having to ask the neighbors to feed me.

I don't want my brother to be smacked around by your boyfriend and when I tell you, you never believe me.

I'm dirty and the other kids make fun of me.

I want you to buy soap but you ask, "What do you want from me?"

I just want you to give me a bath and for you to do my hair.

But, every time I wake up you're elsewhere.

I want you to read with us and for you to teach us our math.

I want to be a happy child because I don't know what it is to laugh.

My teachers ask me am I okay and do I have someone to help.

And give me clothes that they leave on the shelf in the classroom so that I can change.

I'm behind the other kids mommy.

They know division and I can't multiply.

I tell you this everyday but you never try and change.

And I don't want to have to ask my friends mothers for change so that I can get a snack on the way home.

And for once in my life I just want you to stay home.

Stay up.

Not nod in front of us or lay up with that man that I don't like.

I can't spell.

Can you help me to write?

We're in the system now mommy and you have to ask to see us.

We shouldn't have to go through this.

We never asked to be us.

I don't want to have to receive birthday cards in the mail.

Or write letters to jail.

Or have you watch us grow up through pictures.

Or be split up from my brothers and sisters.

I didn’t want to feel like a stranger when I saw you again.

I at least wanted you to show up at my high school graduation even if you never called again.

I don’t want less and I’m more.

I don’t want to hear excuses anymore.

I at least want you to walk me home from school one day or at least try.

I couldn’t see ‘em coming down my eyes.

So I had to make this poem cry.

Effects

Hating that you have such an effect on me.

Causing me not to eat.

So all I do is drink.

Not knowing what to think.

My hand is itching to send you a text.

But I'm trying to avoid doing so.

I'm really having a hard time.

Trying and trying

Crying and crying.

Make up being washed away as soon as it's applied.

I love you enough to let you live.

Favorite

Can I be your favorite poet as I embrace every metaphor with the kiss of a simile?

Or be the iambic pentameter that determines our chemistry?

Can I ease your mind with an acrostic using the letters of your name?

Use repetition to make you feel disdained from the likes of the world?

Drown you with quotes from legendary poets?

I am your Poe, and there was no predicting it.

Decipher me as if reading Dickinson.

Call me Whitman.

But, let me be deep like Giovanni.

Let me be the words to free you.

Poetic protection.

There's no harming thee.

Closure

Call you every morning just to hear the sound of your voice

Sing to you even though I can't sing

Because that's what lovers do

And I would be lying if I told you that I didn't love you

But I'm feeling like our feelings are no longer mutual.

Why be that way when there are no limits to what I'll do for you.

I remember there was a time we would stay on the phone.

But now the conversations have faded and I would rather sit alone.

And ask myself where did everything do a turn around.

When really all I want you to do is turn around.

And look clearly at what's been holding you down.

For this long stretch.

Of time that I wish I could sometimes rewind.

Back to its beginning.

I keep trying when I don't think there's no more trying in me.

All I need is your time and dedication.

And I love you but it differs when it's time that I'm wasting.

On the wrong one.

And I'm questioning if it's you.

Closure is better.

I'm letting you know I'm through.

Playing Second

When it comes to this love thing.
I'm not fully satisfied.
Why?
Many reasons.
But, there's this guy.

He has a woman of his own.
But she isn't holding him down at home.
And I figured a little stepping out with .him wouldn't hurt.
Playing second has it costs.
Knowing you'll never be first.

I see him every day in the cafe'.
We have lunch together and chats about our day.
He is so fine.
That I don't care about the fact he's not mine.
I just thought about what he could do for me.
Not really care for me.
But when I needed the sex he was there for me.

And I would call him in the middle of many nights.
Come through.
Knowing he would have to lie to his wife.
Not once did it cross my mind to put this to an end.
The same man I played second with for years, was the husband of a friend.

Smile Worthy

I didn't know that a smile could be worth so much.

Until today when you embraced me with your touch.

Your kiss I always miss.

When the rain hits or when the sun is shining.

Somehow our time together is always perfect timing.

Your very presence awakens me.

Before my death it's to heaven you've taken me.

Stay with me.

Mental Prison

I watched the sun come up only to sit here on dark nights.

Went to light a cigarette but the flame wouldn't spark right.

Picked up a pen and outlined my life and it was chalk like.

A blurred line that I couldn't make clear.

Times I wanted to cry but couldn't find the tears.

Feeling like I was owed something but couldn't afford the years.

Continued to chase pavements that weren't paved yet.

Lusted over loving people who weren't even saved yet.

Forgot about God in the midst of my troubles.

Remembered all the in vain I love you's.

Stopped to look at my watch but couldn't tell the time.

Became content with the demons around me.

So living in hell was fine.

Poured liquor.

Claimed to be celebrating.

Drowned in sin.

It's myself I'm hating.

Washed my hair and that wasn't enough cleanse.

Looked around and I had lost friends.

Guess they weren't for the long run.

People are only around when it's all fun.

Ran away and said fix it Jesus.

Killed myself in the midst of this agony.

They don't believe it.

Hell and Back

She got her strength back after a major loss.

She put her joy up for sale.

Paying costs, she couldn't afford.

Life was a revolving door.

Split seconds and you didn't see her anymore.

Cleaning up her mess seemed to be a daily chore.

Experiencing so much less.

When she knew she was more.

Queen on her throne but she didn't know how to sit there.

Goals and a dream deferred.

Unsure of how to get there.

Needing a breakthrough.

So she stood in the mirror and said, "Franchesca how long will it take you?"

The mirror responded saying, "Take me wherever you go because you need to see yourself in a better light. You just don't know."

In love with someone who never acknowledged her purpose or reason.

Her hard work and effort for her prosperous season.

She couldn't prosper on her own.

At her best in the company of others.

But, when she's home alone, she's alone in her own skin.

Trying to moisturize her pain but, her skin seemed to crack everyday she lived in shame.

Make up was her wake up but, she couldn't mask it.

Confidence way below average.

Put her faith aside knowing she should've had it.

All the days she experienced the trial of being lost in a world full of anguish and deceit.

When God planted her, he also planted her feet.

To walk a path of strength even when she fell to her knees.

She fell only to get up and try much harder than the time prior.

She was living in hell escaping the fire.

Flying through the flames.

She woke up that day feeling free.

Nothing was the same.

This Too Shall Pass

I'm all in your mind right?

The time you can't sleep at night.

Because you saw your ex for a reason so that you can learn to love yourself.

Sometimes we're at our happiest when we're torn apart.

In between the finish and not knowing where to start.

The slow pumps of blood through cold veins to our heart.

Love is beautiful when everything is okay.

Hell when you wake up and realize they've walked away.

Not from just you but genuine loyalty.

The times I was spoiling you and you were spoiling me.

Wishing you could hold their hand again.

Siting in your room with no one to talk to.

Hoping they'd understand again.

Picture frames empty because you threw the photos away.

They came to get their belongings and you begged them to stay.

Sitting in the car on a summer night watching the rain hit the window shield.

But, your past is your past.

This too shall pass.

This wound will heal.

Complexed

To study the sun to see there's no light.

Apologizing for wrongs never intending to do right.

To stare at the moon when it's full.

You want me to push but you always pull me away from the promises that you never keep.

I always listen but your talk is cheap.

I hear the words you speak but, they never resonate.

I love a lot of people in this world but, for you there's no greater hate.

No, let me take that back.

No greater disposition.

Put in a position that I can't get away from.

You walk all over my feelings and I always run back.

Wishing I could get us back on track.

Because this emotional rollercoaster has run its course.

But of course I'm crazy.

I guess because I express I care for you baby.

Limitations never existed when it came to me and you.

Complexities and being upset you see ain't healthy.

Untitled

I am Bland.

I am I just don't understand.

I am Martin.

I am coffin.

I am Gray.

I am I don't know if this is my last time leaving my house today.

My last time to pray.

I am victim.

I am badge.

The cover up.

I am police.

I do what I want.

You don't know me.

I am no peace.

I am justice unreached.

I am empty clips.

I am gun.

I am shoot that nigger down because he chose to run.

I am choked.

Garner.

I am judged.

Excuse me your honor.

I am judicial.

I am unexcused by government officials.

I am black.

I am thug.

I am fear.

I am rain.

I am storm.

I am someone.

I am human.

I am out of the norm.

Leader

Told I could never be a leader.

Now I'm president.

Trying to come up off of my low.

I haven't been better since.

I'm a keeper as I try to convince myself.

Never a loser because I always ask for help.

I try even though trying hurts sometimes.

When things don't work you still try to make them work sometimes.

I'm a leader.

That's what I tell myself.

I will do my best at all times because no one will hand me anything.

I have to work diligently to reach my goals.

Lead Poisoning

Broke the pencil because I wanted a pen.

Reciting biblical scriptures to get over my sin.

Realized my full potential and all it took was a day.

Needed a blessing and all it took was to pray.

Took off my shoes and just slept in my clothes.

Dreamed of big stages and people supporting my shows.

Mic in my hand world hearing my poems.

On Noah's Ark just steering through storms.

Slingshot through life.

David in the den.

Other than Christ, my savior is my pen.

Woke up again in the middle of the night.

Walking on ink I was inspired to write when it was dark and all I had were words so meaningful.

Writing is my gift when it's just a thing to you.

40 days and 40 writes.

28 years, story of my life.

The genesis and the revelation.

The heaven through hell.

My stanzas escaping.

Earth quaking.

New Addition

I don't want to make love to you.
I want to make love to your spirit.
To you there are depths, so I want to go deep with you.
Be here showing you everything, when all they've offered is to sleep with you.
Understand you at your highs and hold you during your lows.
Stay with you when everyone goes.
When you're sick I'll be there to take care.
When you're asleep I can't help but to stare.
Think about you day and night.
You're so beautiful.
The new addition to my life.

Stage

Packed a box.
Left the keys.
Oh you must didn't believe that I was ready to leave.
You can have the cars, the house and white picket fence.
Vowed my life to you and you've been wicked since.

There's no apology that can put a cover on these feelings of insecurity.
I'm not a cover girl.
And when you look at me I wonder if you see that other girl.

I ran to you but, you've crossed lines..
Not up for competition when I was in it to win.
So I refuse to lose.
You had a choice to hold me down.
But her you chose to choose.
Over our home and solidarity.
Kept lying to my face.
I needed clarity.
To see you with her was what was scaring me.
Dreams and nightmares.
Walked into my kitchen to our children and she happened to be right there.

I should've stayed at work at my desk.
But my intuition said to go home and so did the pain in my chest.
When a woman's fed up, for me it's for life.
As I share this with the audience.
Tears hit the floor.
You're staring at who used to be your wife.

Fear

I'm scared I won't ever get to see your face again.
I'm scared of losing but don't want to end up in a race again.
I'm scared to tell you I love you because I know you don't feel the same.
I'm scared to feel different about you although nothing is the same.

I'm scared to pick up the phone and call you as much.
I'm scared to give you my all and my trust.
I'm scared that everything I think is what you think too.
I'm scared to feel broken into two.

I'm scared that I can't get past old love so I ignore the angel that is so close to my face.
I'm scared I won't have it together and you'll get tired of the wait.

I'm scared because I lied and said that I want you to leave me alone.
Trying to live my own life and take care of my home, be an adult and do what adults do.
But, you stay in the front of my mind.
I've taken advantage of you.

I'm scared because I've lost someone and they can't be replaced.
I cry alone but, really want you to wipe the tears from my face.
I'm scared to really call you back or reply to your messages 'til this very day.
I'm scared God won't answer me.
That's why I never pray.

So to be truthful I see in you what I've never seen in myself.
The joy on your escape.
As I'm denial of help.

I want you to help me be the joyous woman I used to know.
I want to hold on to you when all things go.

I'm scared Franchesca.
I want you to admit that.
Once I'm gone I'm someone you can't get back.

Remain True

Sunshine, all white and heat.
Time is not on our side.
Days so bittersweet.

Wishing I could do a lot of things again and edit mistakes.
Watching my circle closely.
Always aware of the fakes.

Well life you're showing me things I never knew.
Well God I don't know old me because you make all things new.

Franchesca remain true.

Time

Struggle is only temporary.
So I will not become complacent with worry.
Although the unknown is sometimes scary.
I will continue to carry.
Weight dead and alive.
And the struggle to strive.
Along with tears in my eyes.
Along with my pride.
Along with my tries.

Family said Franny you'll never be shit.
God said be faithful and remember never to quit.
Friends said I'll be here through thick and thin.
But, sometimes I question who to really call a friend.
So I depend, solely on Jesus.
I see things clearly when others can never see it.

I chill sit back and watch.
Time isn't on our sides.
All we got is this clock.

Be Free

Dark room because the day has faded away.
Rain storm, I'm afraid so I pray.
But for what?
Every time I try I end up down on my luck.
In love.
No this might very well be lust.
Putting in effort but you never value my trust.

Rubbing my fingers through my hair and singing to myself.
Stressed to the max and this is bad on my health.
Can't even sit at the table to partake in a meal.
Who lied and said all wounds heal?

I bet Jesus still has scars on his skin.
Couldn't walk into my own house comfortably tonight so I crawled in.
Don't believe in half ass anything so that's why I put my all in everything I do.
I mean my everything is you.

But I have to get me back because I'm wet up from the storm I'm afraid of.
To go back to the woman I know I would trade love.
I want freedom again.
I've been a slave love.

The caged bird who sings.
Escaping your ways love.

Be free...

Leading The Blind

They don't believe in you now.
But it will be sooner than later.
The time you swallowed pride and got tired of the favors.

People had their hands out when I could barely feed myself.
Now that I'm back on they're the ones asking for help.

Jesus please be a fence.
I swallow my pride like a bullet and try ignoring my resent for the hollow tips about to pierce my flesh.
Words from the envious.
Wishing they were in my shoes.
Thank you for ordering my steps.

I roll with different crews.
Just to be receptive of different views.
On how to make it through the times when nobody has your back.
Or when they say she'll be nothing and lurk on my Facebook asking where my status at.

Well I'm logged in and charged up.
And I ain't dying.
The pen is always working.
And I ain't lying.
In the lions den and I ain't lion.

Leading the blind.
Ain't no free in my time.

Choose

I can find anyone to lay with me.
But I need someone with substance and plans to stay with me.

I don't talk just for you to listen but to have a response.
I respect who you are but dislike who you aren't.

I can no longer put everything on hold for you.
You said that you have a focus.
I have a focus too.

You said you want different but settle for the same things
You want temporary and I'm forever.
I want your last name.
You're playing the same game she played with you.
I'm much smarter I'll leave before I'll be in this to lose.
You have to choose.

13 Steps

A picture that hung from a nail on my wall.
You.
The time I know to take it down is now.
True.
You don't deserve to live in my space.
I'd rather that part of the house to be empty.
I thought before this love thing we had a friendship.
But, you're not all that friendly.

Stairs.
I couldn't catch my balance as you threw me down 13 memories.

1 -The same violence I witnessed displayed on the face of my mother.
2- The calls as my father begged to come back each time saying all he did was love her.
3- Me standing in the window because it always seemed to rain.
4- Running to hide because the screams had gotten to loud.
5- Daddy playing the music over my mother's cries for help.
6- My bookcase tipping over as my heart fell from the shelves.
7- Looking at my face at age 9 and realizing I looked like mommy before daddy had done that to her face.
8- The 911 call I had to make.
9- Sitting on the closet floor telling the operator mommy isn't moving anymore.
10- Me going to shake her as she lost life in her limbs.
11- Looking at you and realize you resembled him. My dad.
12- Hitting the last step. Suddenly in shock.
13- Getting up to leave because my mother could not.

All These Questions

When you die, is it really alone?
When you step into your house, is it really your home?
Why is money the reason we work so hard?
Why was the Bible written?
Why do we believe in God?
Why do people do life in prisons?
Why do people get killed or come up missing?
Who is the leader of the crop?
Why do gang initiations exist and when will they stop?
Why isn't the Revolution televised?
Why weren't the reporters at the Million Man March yesterday?
Why am I not surprised?
Why is change sometimes uncomfortable?
Why is the struggle real and I can't afford to do all the things I want to do?
Why are people dying of starvation?
Why are people complacent instead of dream chasing?
Why was there slavery for 300+ years?
Is Africa really the mother land?
Why does racism divide us as a people?
Why does weaponry exist?
And why is it lethal?
Why do I have to work 40 hours every week?
When the world ends, will it start over again?
So many questions from the point of my pen.

Sleep Walking

Awakened from my sleep with the thought of you on my mind.
Looked at the clock but didn't recognize the time.
Stared in the mirror and my skin was puffy around the eyes.
Missing you every day I try not to cry.

Laid back down only to get up again.

Was thirsty so I went downstairs to fill my cup again.
Walked up the steps and stood in the hallway.
Life is difficult and a lot of times we'll learn lessons the hard way.

Heard my phone ring but it wasn't a call from you.
And now I'm back in bed legs shaking and confused.
Alarm went off.
Not feeling work so I hit snooze.

As much as I don't want you to go.
I know this isn't about me.
Trying not to sound selfish.
I'll send this to you and let you be.
You might not say anything.
But at least you took the time to read.

For You

From the beginning I told you that I'll compromise for you
Dry your eyes for you
And every time I turn around these tears drop from my eyes for you

I'm waiting for you
Shots to the head so I won't feel these lonely feelings I'm taking for you
I'm blatant for you
Heart aching for you
Arrow to the arteries I'm shaking for you

My love is rainforest fresh for you
Even at my worst I strive to put forward my best for you
Heart skips beats in my chest for you
Always thinking more never less for you

Strive for you
Stay alive for you
You be the seek and I be the hide for you

Be the art for you.
The muse for you.
The paint for you.
What others ain't for you.

The sky and clouds for you.
The verbs, nouns and adjectives spoken aloud for you.
The poems for you.
The survivor of the fittest through storms for you.

The raindrops for you.
Standing tall this is where pain stops for you.

The medicine for you.
Deadly weapon for you.
All this time and I've been destined for you.

She Is

She plans for her future.
As she drives past her past.
Road blocks tumbling through her rear view glass.

She is the revolution of every day.
She is the sun in every ray.
She is the tear drop that never hit the ground.
She is loud in her travels never making a sound.

She is copper before gold.
She is truth before it ever gets told.
She is tall sometimes falling short.
She is the defendant of her own court.

She is the photo without its elements.
She is heaven with no hell in it.
She is awake living in a dream.
She is the needle that pulls into seams.

She is golden although sometimes blue.
I look in the mirror sometimes asking, "Franchesca is that you?"

I want to see my son live before he's even conceived.
I don't want him to be a black corpse laying in these
streets.
I want him to wear his hoodie with pride and walk through
gated communities without fear.
I want him to walk when he sees the police.
I want him to be confident in his everyday life.
His life already matters.

I Hope

I hope that for every time you stared at your phone when I called you felt better about it.
I hope that for every time you saw my face it actually altered your feelings.
I hope that every poem I've ever sent you is of actual healing.
I hope that one day you meet someone you actually care about.
Tell them the truth and stick by them no matter the circumstance.
Not settle for less of anything by happenstance.
I hope that I'll get over you soon because it's getting late.
I hope that when you read this you realize in my heart you have a place.

I can't give up.

I won't chase pavements.

I will stand strong.

Never a conformist of hatred.

I will love all no matter the place nor time.

I will make changes starting with self, then extending my hand to all mankind.

She walks with her head down because she never felt on a high.

She never knew the truth because all her life she's been told lies.

She never liked to read because every character seemed to be her.

She liked to swim until that day she got in the pool and drowned.

She is writers block.

Floating amongst clouds.

Voice with no sound.

Read This

If I never write a poem again somebody read this to God, the Pope, the Pastors.
We're living in modern day slavery.
So read it to the masters.
Or the black statistic from years ago soon to get his masters.

To the young thug who always seems to be black with no focus.
To a writer like myself who is unstable but potent.
To the trees with our ancestors blood stains.
The KKK.
They probably hand us our jobs because we never know who hides behind those white sheets.
That's a gang too right?
Just on horses with clean getaways.

The teachers and professors.
How about Obama's predecessor?
To your son or daughter who needs to know what all of this is about.
The fields slaves used to work in.
The same fields of today experiencing droughts.

Baltimore City, Compton and the Chi.
The children with no meals fighting every day to survive.
My friends daughter who was shot in a corner store just thinking of a snack.
My dad who was held up at gunpoint for his ATM withdrawal.
The minds going crazy but they want us to pretend to be cordial.

Read this to the history the white man is afraid to televise.
Somebody read this to that reporter from CNN last April standing on Penn North telling lies.
He knew nothing about the city but made it sound so corrupt.

I guess Freddie Gray's death was supposed to be on a hush.
Too much publicity right?
All these journalists want to write about is when the city has lost another life.
So read this to them.
Read this to every politician still holding the ball but never make the shot for us so we fall off the rim.
To the drug dealers who only care about their Jordan money bread, butter and Tims.
Somebody read this to every homeless man in Baltimore.
Tell them to press forward because there's always more.

Read this to the churches in the pulpit.
They don't need a sermon today.
Why?
Because I have something to say.

Read this to the entire nation.
At every celebration.
Funerals, birthdays, worst days.
I just felt good but I'm down bad.
Read this on my hurt days.
Don't throw this away.
Read this before you pray.

Even when I'm dead and rotten, read this to every poet in America
I shall not be forgotten.

Can’t Be The Only One

Sometimes I don't feel like forgiving.
Sometimes I don't feel like being forgiven.
Sometimes I don't want to be free.
Sometimes I want to be imprisoned.
Sometimes I keep quiet and just think the things I want to say.
Sometimes I don't believe in God.
Sometimes I don't pray.
Sometimes I'm fearful of tomorrow.
What if it doesn't come?
Sometimes I feel dead alive.
I can't be the only one.

Lines Of Symmetry

Considered an outcast because I outlast dreams deferred.
Poet deep in sin I expose you kings and queens to words.
Sunshine when thunder hits.
Keep going when you want to quit.
Poetic lines of symmetry.
Molecular phrases.
Poetic chemistry.
The blueprint or the holy grail.
Words are my freedom.
I will never see a jail.

Hopeless Romantics

Hopeless romantics who don't believe in romances.
Just love at risk.
Slits in wrists.
Bad chicks.
Gun clips and fun shit.
With one wish.
To be different than differences.
No plans or specific shit.
Robbing hearts of blood pumps.
On some hit list shit.
Running away but end in the same place.
At the finish line of life.
At the start of heavens gates.

Wish List

I wish we didn't have to die alone.
I wish I could bring back my homie who was shot down not even a block from his home.
I wish my girlfriend didn't have to be scared to walk into her home without being smacked.
I wish I could turn on the TV and not see all these homicide stats.
I wish that teen student Arnesha Bowers from City College High wasn't a victim of a gang initiation.
I wish Travis Dixon could've shown face at his high school reunion.
I wish Freddie Gray would've walked that day and not ran.
I wish Baltimore didn't look like LA Riots in April.
I wish that little boy could go home from school each day to a meal on his table.
I wish Damon Jennings could've made it back to Baltimore and not left dead in the woods by his friends.
I wish we really knew the people we call friends.
I wish Trayvon Martin would've walked a different way from the corner store.
I wish I didn't feel like my brothers are a target in these streets.
I wish Kendal Fenwick could have raised his children somewhere further than Park Heights, so in that instance 8 days after his 25th birthday he wouldn't have lost his life.
I wish my grandmother could remember me.
I wish I didn't feel like resulting to drugs sometimes.
I wish I didn't sit in a dark room needing love sometimes.
I wish those families in Haiti didn't have to survive off of dirt cookies.
I wish most of what I worked for wasn't taken in taxes.
I wish worth wasn't broken down into tax brackets.
I wish the Bible was written in the hood.
I wish Sandra Bland would've made it home from those prison walls.
I wish Tyshawn Lee wasn't another baby boy gone too soon.

I wish marriage wasn't publicized as much.
I wish you weren't judged because of your sexual preference.
I wish true love wasn't hard to find.
I wish I could open the eyes of the blind.
I wish my church member didn't lose her life last Saturday due to a drunk driver.
I wish everyone knew God for themselves.
I wish these weren't the last days.
I wish the homeless didn't have to fight to survive every day and night.
I wish police brutality wasn't so common in 2016.
I wish I didn't have to question whether my brother will make it out of his teens.
I wish hip hop still had substance.
I wish I didn't have to abide by the systematic laws of this corrupted government.
I wish equality was really demonstrated.
I wish my loc'd hair didn't say unprofessional to the white man.
I wish I could feel safe wherever I go.
I wish we could sit down at a table Indian style and just pray.
I wish the deaf could hear what I have to say.
I wish everywhere I looked I didn't read 'Pray For Paris' today
I wish I could fly away with God's son.
I wish that when it's time for my autopsy they find every poem I've ever written in the center of my lungs.

You ever wonder where life is about to take you?

Don't judge her.

She's gaining her strength back.

She's becoming tall again.

So that when obstacles present themselves, on her face she doesn't fall again.

Love Is

Love is a high.
When it's good anyway.
Love is, we're having problems so let's get on our knees and pray.
Love is the power to understand.
Love is patience wrapped in kindness.
Love is strength.
Love is weakness.
Love is support.
Love is unconditional.
Love is being a friend.
Love is unafraid.
Love is brave.
Love is courageous.
Love is pride.
Love is smiles.
Love is crying and laughing all in the same.
Love is giving.
Love is addition.
Love is you.
Love is me.
Love is so much more than so many things we see.

Storyteller

I'm goin' write a story.
You may not like my story.
It could be about freedom or prison.
You know a Rikers story.

I'm going to drink my wine and listen to Sade'.
Roll these dice of life like it's all play.
Do one thing repetitively like I have all day.

Going to shoot my veins to feel the adrenaline rush to my brain.
I'm going to fold my arms as if in a stray jacket with no restraint.
Sniff cocaine until I overdose.
And meet Jehovah's ghost in heaven.
I'm sorry the middle of hell.
As I dance in this pool of holy water.
Oh life was swell.

Hair Thing

If every woman wanted to be Beyonce', would there be Jill Scotts?
Heads full of natural hair.
Women who embrace their knots.

I am not my hair.
You really are.
When you flat iron it and damage it with grease.
Don't go bald and decide to glue in a piece.
Eyelashes longer than your nails.
Hurry up to make that Brazilian sale.

Girl leave your hair alone.
It's fine.
Whoever told you that you need all that was a waste of your time.

The next time you go to a beauty store the first thing you should pick up is a mirror.
It will reflect the woman God made you to be.
Your true beauty never lies.
The truth will be much clearer.

THE ONLY CHAPTER

Be

I am locked up in a world full of pain.
Where is my release?
I want you to correct me behind these bars of imprisonment.
Life is a gamble.
Isn't it?

My body is sacred but I want you to unwrap my cloth.
Unwrap it like I've been underground for centuries but discovered again after being lost.
Take me out of my box and make me anew.
Give me life all over.
Be my pallbearer lifting me on your shoulder.
But, lift me up never letting me down.
Lifeguard me for I don't want to drown.

Guide me and be my counselor.
Let me drink from your water.
I'm thirsty for every ounce of you.

Be my yoga instructor and have me bend for you.
Make me feel like forever.
I want no end with you.

Plans

I be wanting to relax with you.

Turn off the TV and music.

Just have an open conversation and take it back with you.

Get stacks with you.

Never have to ask of you.

Paint with you.

Have patience and be what others ain't for you.

And I'm thanking you for all that you plan to do.

You didn't know but I'm telling you now that I have a plan for you.

To be a wife to you.

Always write to you.

This is temporary air.

I've decided to pray for eternal life with you.

No Evidence

She hangs from rope.

He bangs and sells dope.

She is victim of rape.

He measures life from a tape.

Yellow aka caution.

Dead bodies outlined in chalk and blood.

She seeks love from strangers.

He keeps all anger inside.

She retreats to corners as way to survive.

He throws money.

She be best buy.

He be key to that ride.

She fantasize.

No fruition.

No tuition.

Mind to waste.

Gun to brain.

Pulled trigger.

Called insane.

Suicidal.

But, Jesus was idol.

I mean Bible.

Ancient pages.

He wrote about her.

Poems shared on stages.

No way out.

Words be his mazes.

She be his scripture.

He be painted picture.

They be acquainted quitters.

So they inhale pounds.

Drink to melodic sounds.

Shoot up in swimming pools.

Then drown.

Later then found with crowns and crosses around the necks of them.

Yes they lost it.

They didn't find their way back.

Yellow tape reads caution.

No evidence of tracks.

Too Deep For You To Understand

The teacher teaches and the pastor preaches.

To set goals far past your reach is what makes sense.

But, somehow it's all about what makes cents to calculate to dollars.

And if you ain't on six figure level it's forget you from the government.

They'll holler at you when it's time for you to reap benefits you've sown all your life.

And if you've never invested in a 401K then I guess it's social security.

Hold on.

I don't know if y'all hearing me.

'Cause I don't want y'all to just be reading me.

But, I'm the only one feeding me and when it comes to this money, these white people are cheating me.

Working me like a slave telling me I'm housekeeping see.

No complaints but tell it like it is.

Place me on a platform and place your bids.

Call him master as he rapes your kids.

Drink from the fountain and call her colored.

Throw them in a section and call it 8.

Sick that black meat.

There is no escape from the project set forth.

And although it's been manifest in the courts that equality is a right,
I beg to differ.

And forget a right 'cause my opinion is never wrong.

Same job 10 years and there's no seniority.

Bring the white kids in.

I train them and still they make more than me.

Best employee yet my check doesn't say so.

I don't live a monopoly life so I don't expect play dough.

But, you know what they say go from the time of Willie Lynch.

Never wanting us to know what they know.

That's why I take advantage of my ability to write.

I observe and place words on paper.

Freedom.

My daughter.

You can never take her and give her another name but speech.

Lift every voice.

I’m the star on the banner.

Brown me.

Too deep to understand her.

Ruined Reputation

She's twerking for some change.

Still worthless in the brain.

She 'bout to go insane.

She never asked his name.

See she never asked his name.

On stage she was a star.

Off stage she hid behind scars of ruined reputation.

Club life she became complacent with its setting.

She seemed to be forgetting that you go down, you hoe now.

No slow down.

They know now what it does because it didn't take but a few shots to see what it do.

A few dollars and you loving the crew.

But you never loved you.

Trust issues are real.

These men will never trust you.

They will only fuck you.

Place everything above you.

Suck you and say fuck you.

Lust too.

Nothing left but that money at the end of your nights.

Shaking nude in those flashing lights.

It's a way to live the lavish life but, your way is the hardest.

Regardless of anything else, you've made a name for yourself.

That's the young woman with no class.

All because you didn't want a 9 to 5.

Stop shaking your ass.

Reinstated

Love.

I can't shake you.

Can't replace you.

Wanting to embrace you, I look for ways to mold and shape you.

You are my prison bars.

I can't escape you.

You are the poetry on my paper.

I could never erase you.

We've had falling outs but, I want to reinstate you.

Climb mountain peaks for you.

Put away the streets for you.

Sit at an empty table and always find a way to eat with you.

Last one I call at night.

The first one I see in the morning sunlight.

One I give my last to.

Even if that means breath,

Saying I love you as the oxygen leaves my chest.

History

Years of good and bad.

Yet the bad outweighs the good.

Leaving you a long time ago was something that I didn't think I could.

But now it's time to let go of all these negative thoughts that cross my mind every day.

The internal debate of walking away when I really don't want to leave you behind.

Knowing that my love for you has had its vacancy and staying because of complacency is when you'll start hating me.

I'm not going to blame everything on you.

Shit happens and I've done wrong too.

Our love making has turned to just a cum for me and I cum for you.

No four play.

Pull out and you're through.

What about my body you've always caressed?

Before us going to sleep we'd get everything off our chest.

Feelings have become bottled.

Everything just hit me full throttle.

I wanted to carry my first child for you.

I remember walking into our home and it being something your smile would do.

Now I have to ask for your kiss.

Your insecure ass is always asking questions like who am I with.

Just know it isn't you.

I'm not cheating but, I'm fed up and there's nothing you can do.

Just be respectful.

Pack your things and leave.

Let history be history.

I'm no longer naïve.

Diary Entry

See you at the crossroads because I've been heaven sent.

To live in a place, you haven't been.

Don't worry about me.

I'm somewhere in the clouds.

To everyone here staring at me for the last time I hope I've made you proud.

12 gates and pearls.

Some of you don't see md in a deathly state but as a little girl.

I don't want y'all to miss me at all.

Just prepare yourselves for your final call.

Death for me is easy.

Life had been so complex.

Worked so much only to live check to check.

Never paid what I was worth.

Bruised and bitter because of a man whom I couldn't stay with.

Hurt.

Played victim in my home from the time I was 8.

Dad decided it would be my sanity he would take.

Rape.

Touch it but don't tell a soul stuck with me until I accepted Christ.

Then I forgave that man because I didn't want to live in guilt.

Became ill.

Thank you all for coming to my bedside on my last days.

Meant a lot even though I was never able to express what each of you meant to me personally.

I wish you could hear me now.

I'm reciting my poems to the harps of angels and getting fitted for my crown.

See you later.

I'm in heaven now.

Poetry has had me mature and develop as a young woman. I never used to think that I could write about so much until I read Medicinal Wordplay. I hope that you've gained something from reading this book. A lot of the poems come from a personal space. I talk about my life experiences in a lot of them. Also, as I thought about the content itself I instantly thought of you. Yes you! We may not know each other personally but at some point or another I've talked specifically about your story in one of my poems. These poems are meant to be your medicine. You've just had a dose of poetry that will heal you for life. Thank you for reading!

With Unconditional Love,

Franchesca Collins

Made in the USA
Middletown, DE
05 February 2023

23544161R00096